OXFORD BACH BOOKS FOR ORGAN

MANUALS ONLY
BOOK 1

Compiled and edited by Anne Marsden Thomas

with Notes by Russell Stinson

MUSIC DEPARTMENT

OXFORD
UNIVERSITY PRESS

OXFORD
UNIVERSITY PRESS

Great Clarendon Street, Oxford OX2 6DP,
United Kingdom

Oxford University Press is a department of the University of Oxford.
It furthers the University's objective of excellence in research, scholarship,
and education by publishing worldwide. Oxford is a registered trade mark of
Oxford University Press in the UK and in certain other countries

© Oxford University Press 2014

Anne Marsden Thomas has asserted her right under the Copyright, Designs
and Patents Act, 1988, to be identified as the Editor of this Work

Database right Oxford University Press (maker)

First published 2014

Impression: 7

ISBN 978-0-19-338673-0

Music and text origination by Katie Johnston

Printed in Great Britain on acid-free paper by
Halstan & Co. Ltd, Amersham, Bucks.

Contents

Introduction

The five volumes in this graded anthology aim to provide reliable editions with minimal editorial intervention for this cornerstone of the organ repertoire. With informative Notes on the Pieces from a renowned Bach scholar, practical notes on style and technique, and suggested fingering and footing for selected pieces from each volume available online, the series aims to provide all the resources required by a player in their first years of exploring the organ works of Bach.

Two books in the set are for manuals only and three for manuals and pedals. The volumes reflect the grades of the Associated Board of the Royal Schools of Music as follows: Manuals Only: Book 1 Grades 2–5; Book 2 Grades 5–8; Manuals and Pedals: Book 1 Grades 4–6; Book 2 Grades 6–7; Book 3 Grades 7–8. Within each book pieces are presented in progressive order of difficulty, though this is occasionally interrupted to vary the sequence of pieces or to avoid impractical page turns.

All suitable pieces with a BWV number were considered for inclusion (those few now acknowledged to have been composed by others are identified in the Notes on the Pieces). Most of the pieces were originally composed for organ, though in the Manuals Only books a few pieces for other keyboard instruments that work well on the organ have also been included. The first book in each set also offers some of Bach's harmonizations of Lutheran chorales. As well as being enjoyable to play, these offer valuable studies in touch and introduce the player to the inspiration for many of the organ works. For all chorale preludes included in the anthology, the Notes provide the chorale melody and the first stanza of the text in the original German with an English translation.

Editorial principles

Two important principles governed the editing: to present the pieces as clearly as possible, facilitating reading and hence performance, and to preserve the integrity of the part-writing so that contrapuntal lines are clear. Where these two principles were in conflict we have usually favoured the first, distributing the notes carefully between the hands, either by changing their staves or by providing brackets to indicate the hand to be used, whichever system best enables the player to respond to both the practical arrangements and the musical voice leading.

Bach and his copyists used fermata signs (but inconsistently) to mark the ends of phrases in chorale preludes. We have omitted all fermatas used for this purpose. This may seem a radical decision, but we have applied fermatas to all phrase-ends in the chorales given in the Notes. Players should begin by exploring the chorale phrases in the Notes and then analyse the chorale's behaviour in the piece.

All editorial ornaments, dynamics, and performance suggestions are shown in square brackets. Editorial ornaments have been kept to an absolute minimum so that organists can learn for themselves where ornaments might be inserted.

Baroque scores display a variety of signs to indicate the trill. In order to avoid confusing students, all trills in these anthologies use ⟿ (see No. 1 in Bach's table of ornaments on page 5). Most trills should end as in No. 1 of this table, but some may end as in No. 3, especially if the final two notes of a trill's closing mordent appear as full notes in the score. Editorial notes are cue-sized.

Articulation marks are only included where original. Cautionary accidentals have sometimes been added for clarity. In order to avoid cluttering the score, we have used only very sparingly diagonal rules to show the movement of a part between staves. If a single note is sounded simultaneously in two or more voices, we have usually added round brackets to the note which need not be played.

Technique and Performance

Although this anthology does not primarily aim to be a training method, its users may appreciate a few remarks about appropriate technique and performance (see also the books listed in the Bibliography on page 5).

Posture

Reports of Bach's own playing indicate that his hands and arms stayed still while his fingers remained on the keys: according to the German theorist and composer Johann Philipp Kirnberger, 'one could scarcely see his fingers moving' (in Sulzer's *Allgemeine Theorie der schönen Kunste*, 1774). However, the lower body must be free to turn so that the knees usually hover above, or even anticipate the position of the feet.

Touch

The default keyboard touch in Bach's day was very slightly detached. This touch was repeatedly described by Bach's contemporaries, for example by Marpurg in his *Anleitung zum Clavierspielen*, 1765:

Both legato and staccato are quite distinct from the 'normal way' ['das ordentliche Fortgehen'], in which the finger is very quickly raised from the previous key just before the following note is touched. The normal way is always implied and therefore never explicitly marked.

However, organists should remember two further points about touch:
1. Bach recommended on the title-pages of the Inventions (1723) a singing style of playing;
2. Ornaments are played *legato*, so slurs should be applied to ornaments; additionally, slurs, or near-slurs, may often be applied to ornamental figures that occur within the beat.

Articulation

The attack and release of the note potentially carries much expression. A larger break before rhythmically or otherwise musically important notes (for example, the first note of the beat, climactic chords) is usually appropriate, so that the 'consonant' which starts the note can be heard more vividly. Organists should control, coordinate, and carefully time the release of notes, listening intently to their effect.

Fingering and footing
Larger articulation breaks are useful opportunities to change the position of the hand. Thus the hand always remains comfortable but, in the articulation breaks, it frequently shifts to a new position. At the start of a new hand position it may be wise to pencil in the first finger used, thus identifying a hand position which allows easy access to all the notes until the next articulation break.

Almost no detail is known about Bach's pedalling technique, but the tradition, the design of pedal-boards and benches, and, most of all, the pedal parts themselves suggest playing almost entirely with toes only, with much use of alternate toes.

Marking scores
Players will benefit enormously from marking the fingering and footing into their scores. As C. P. E. Bach wrote 'At the keyboard almost anything can also be played with a wrong fingering, although with prodigious difficulty and awkwardness' (*Versuch über die wahre Art das Clavier zu spielen*, 1753, Chapter 1.3). As preparation, we recommend that organists first study the individual voice parts in isolation, as this will reveal the shape of the line and points of articulation and hence the most appropriate fingering and pedalling. Extracts of a few pieces from these anthologies with fingering and footing added are provided as an online resource to guide players – visit the *Oxford Bach Books for Organ* pages of **www.oup.com/uk** and click on the link to the online resources.

Registration
Bach sometimes gave brief directions regarding registration, for example *pro Organo pleno* and *à 2 claviers*, and these have been reproduced in this book. Reports of Bach's playing confirm that his registrations were innovative, but unfortunately no details survive. Much has been written elsewhere about Bach's probable registration practices (see the books recommended below), so we give here only a few practical starting-points.
- Play both hands on the same manual unless otherwise indicated, or unless one hand has a solo voice.
- If the pedal has a solo part (e.g. a chorale tune) register it first, then choose manual stops to balance. Otherwise register manuals first, then (usually) choose similar stops for the pedal an octave lower.
- Fugues and their Preludes were probably played on *Organo pleno*, a big chorus of Principal stops on manual and pedal plus Reed(s) in pedal (i.e. Manual 16', 8', 4', 2⅔', 2', Mixture; Pedal 32', 16', 8', 4', Reeds 16', 8'). This chorus may be reduced in smaller-scale pieces (e.g. avoid the manual 16' and pedal 32' if more clarity is needed).
- Never couple the manual that is being used to the pedal, unless there is no alternative. If there are too few pedal stops to balance the manual, try coupling down a manual not being used.
- For greatest clarity, use only one stop of each pitch.

Ornamentation
Organists should consider adding cadential ornaments where the music seems to invite this. Other ornaments may be added as appropriate, but never at the expense of the musical line or technical control.

The following is J. S. Bach's table of ornaments from his *Clavierbüchlein vor Wilhelm Friedemann Bach* (1720) written for his then ten-year-old son:

Explanation of various signs, showing how to play certain ornaments correctly:

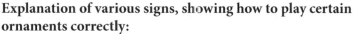
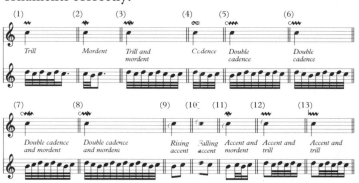

Acknowledgements

These books gained enormously from the expertise and inspiration of David Blackwell, Head of Music Publishing at OUP until 2013. To Professor Russell Stinson I owe a great debt of gratitude for his enlightening Notes. I am grateful for the help of James Hardiker who translated the chorale texts. Throughout the preparation of these books I have been immensely fortunate in having the unending support and patient good sense of my husband Dr Brian Solomons.

Anne Marsden Thomas
London, January, 2014

Bibliography

Technique and Performance
Booth, Colin. *Did Bach really mean that? Deceptive Notation in Baroque Keyboard Music.* Soundboard, 2011.

Faulkner, Quentin. *J. S. Bach's Keyboard Technique.* Concordia, 1984.

Laukvik, Jon. *Historical Performance Practice in Organ Playing, Baroque and Classical Period.* Carus-Verlag, 1996.

Oortmerssen, Jacques van. *Organ Technique.* GOArt Publications, No. 9. Göteborg University, 2002.

Soderlund, Sandra. *How did they play? How did they teach?: A History of Keyboard Technique.* Hinshaw Music, 2006.

Registration
Faulkner, Quentin. *The Registration of Bach's Organ Music.* Wayne Leupold Editions, 2008.

Owen, Barbara. *The Registration of Baroque Organ Music.* Indiana University Press, 1997.

Wolff, Christoph, Butler, Lynn, and Zepf, Marcus. *The Organs of J. S. Bach: A Handbook.* University of Illinois Press, 2012.

1. Liebster Immanuel

(Dearest Immanuel)

BWV 485

2. O Jesulein süss, o Jesulein mild

(Sweet Jesus, gentle Jesus)

BWV 493

3. Jesu, meines Herzens Freud

(Jesus, joy of my heart)

BWV 473

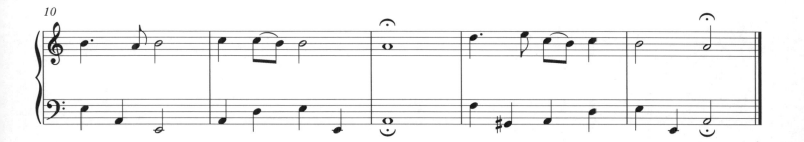

4. Ich hab mein Sach Gott heimgestellt

(I have put all my affairs in the hands of God)

BWV 708

BWV 708a

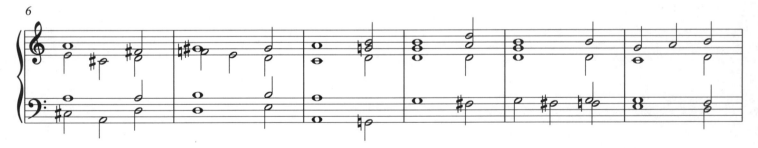

5. Allein Gott in der Höh sei Ehr

(We honour only God on high)

4 (25)

8 (29)

12 (33)

16 (37)

19 (40)

6. Prelude in C minor

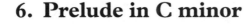

BWV 934

7. Ich halte treulich still

(I wait quietly and faithfully)

BWV 466

8. Prelude in D minor

BWV 935

9. Dir, dir, Jehovah, will ich singen

(To you, Jehovah, I will sing)

BWV 452

10. Bourrée I

from *Overture in the French Style*

11. Herr Christ, der einig Gottes Sohn

(Lord Christ, the only Son of God)

BWV 698

12. Prelude in D major

BWV 936

13. Nun ruhen alle Wälder

(All the forests are resting)

BWV 756

14. Lob sei dem allmächtigen Gott

(Praise to almighty God)

BWV 704

15. Nun freut euch, lieben Christen gmein

(Dear Christians, let us rejoice together)

BWV 755

16. Prelude in C major

BWV 943

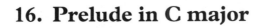

17. Fughetta in G major

BWV 902

18. Herr Jesu Christ, dich zu uns wend

(Lord Jesus Christ, turn to us)

BWV 726

19. Allein Gott in der Höh sei Ehr

(We honour only God on High)

The final four staccato dots of the second and third entries are editorial.

20. Nun freut euch, lieben Christen gmein

(Dear Christians, let us rejoice together)

BWV 734

21. Adagio

2nd movement of Concerto in A minor, after Vivaldi

BWV 593

22. Vater unser im Himmelreich

(Our Father in heaven)

BWV 683

23. Wer nur den lieben Gott lässt walten

(Whoever surrenders control to God alone)

BWV 691

24. Wer nur den lieben Gott lässt walten

(Whoever surrenders control to God alone)

25. Erbarm dich mein, o Herre Gott

(Have pity on me, O Lord God)

BWV 721

26. Wer nur den lieben Gott lässt walten

(Whoever surrenders control to God alone)

BWV 690

4 (14)

7 (17)

20

24 (34)

28 (38)

27. Christum wir sollen loben schon

(We shall praise Christ)

BWV 696

28. Nun komm, der Heiden Heiland

(Come, saviour of the heathens)

BWV 699

29. Vater unser im Himmelreich

(Our Father in heaven)

BWV 737

30. Jesus, meine Zuversicht

(Jesus, who is my assurance)

BWV 728

31. Gelobet seist du, Jesu Christ

(Let us praise you, Jesus Christ)

BWV 722

32. Gelobet seist du, Jesu Christ

(Let us praise you, Jesus Christ)

BWV 697

33. Vom Himmel hoch, da komm ich her

(I have come down from heaven above)

BWV 701

34. Herzliebster Jesu, was hast du verbrochen

(Beloved Jesus, what wrong have you done)

BWV 1093

35. Allegro

1st movement of Concerto in F major, after Vivaldi

[Tutti]

[Solo]

[Tutti]

[Tutti]

[Solo]

[Tutti]

[Tutti]

[Solo]

[Tutti]

36. Fugue in C major

BWV 952

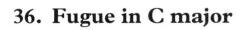

Appendix: Fugue in G minor

(Lass mich gehn, denn dort kommt meine Mutter her*)

Johann Georg Schübler

* See note on p. 63.

Notes on the Pieces

Russell Stinson

Notes have not been provided for the simple chorale harmonizations (Nos. 1–3, 7, and 9).

4. Ich hab mein Sach Gott heimgestellt, BWV 708 and 708a

Ich hab mein Sach Gott heim- gestellt,	I have put all my affairs in the hands of God,
Er machs mit mir, wies ihm gefällt.	So that he may do whatever he wishes with me.
Soll ich allhier noch länger leben, Ohn Widerstrebn	If I am given longer to live here, I will not resist
Seim Willen tu ich mich ergebn.	As I submit to his will.

Johann Leon, 1589

These modest works—conceived perhaps for voices rather than solo organ—should be understood not as different versions of the same composition but as different harmonizations of the same chorale. Their authenticity has been questioned, but both are ascribed to Bach in a manuscript now known to have been copied by Carl Gotthelf Gerlach, a colleague and possibly a student of Bach's in Leipzig. The high incidence of diminished-seventh chords suggests an early composition date, perhaps no later than 1700.

5. Allein Gott in der Höh sei Ehr, BWV 711

Allein Gott in der Höh sei Ehr Und Dank für seine Gnade,	We honour only God on high And thank him for the mercy he shows,
Darum dass nun und nimmermehr Uns rühren kann kein Schade. Ein Wohlgefalln Gott an uns hat, Nun ist gross Fried ohn Unterlass, All Fehd hat nun ein Ende.	Because now and for ever We are protected from all harm. God is pleased with us, Now there is great peace for ever, All hostility has come to an end.

Nicolaus Decius, 1523

There are more organ settings by Bach of this chorale, whose text paraphrases the 'Gloria in excelsis Deo' from the Latin Mass, than any other. In this two-voice arrangement, or bicinium, the right hand takes the hymn tune, while vigorous figuration in the left hand serves as a ritornello, or returning theme. Replete with fast arpeggios and wide leaps, this cello-like melody also alludes to the first phrase of the chorale. Little wonder that such an engaging theme inspired Johannes Brahms in the writing of his organ chorale 'Herzlich tut mich erfreuen', Op. 122, No. 4.

6. Prelude in C minor, BWV 934

This prelude, together with the Prelude in D minor, BWV 935

(No. 8), and the Prelude in D major, BWV 936 (No. 12), comes from Bach's so-called *Six Little Preludes*, BWV 933–8, a collection based on ascending keys (C-c-d-D-E-e) that may or may not have been assembled by the composer himself. According to Johann Nikolaus Forkel (1802), Bach drafted the preludes for his legions of pupils. All six works exemplify binary form, with a double bar at the midpoint.

The C minor prelude so closely matches the Courante from Bach's second French Suite for harpsichord that it may at one time have been intended as a movement within that composition. Not only are the figuration and harmonies remarkably similar, but the texture (in two voices), form, metre, and tonality are the same as well. In an opening gesture reminiscent of Antonio Vivaldi, bars 1–4 establish the C minor tonality, and bars 5–8 feature modulatory, sequential figuration via the circle of fifths. Two-voice texture likewise characterizes the D minor prelude, except that the counterpoint there is imitative, just as in Bach's Two-Part Invention in D minor, which has the same time signature and rhythmic profile to boot. In this prelude the composer has created an arithmetically balanced design whose two halves consist exactly of twenty-four bars each. What distinguishes the D major prelude from the preceding two is the presence of a third voice. As the walking bass and chains of suspensions also demonstrate, the Italian trio sonata as codified by Arcangelo Corelli served as Bach's exemplar.

8. Prelude in D minor, BWV 935

See note to No. 6.

10. Bourrée I, from *Overture in the French Style*, BWV 831

Published in 1735, and a rare example of a Bach work printed during his own lifetime, the *Overture in the French Style* consists of a French overture, nine dances, and a concluding Echo. Its first bourrée exhibits the two defining traits of that dance: duple metre and a quarter-bar anacrusis. Within the context of a perfectly symmetrical binary form, two-voice texture obtains, as in so many of the composer's essays in this dance type.

11. Herr Christ, der einig Gottes Sohn, BWV 698

Herr Christ, der einig Gottes Sohn, Vaters in Ewigkeit, Aus seim Herzen entsprossen, Gleichwie geschrieben steht, Er is der Morgensterne, Sein Glänzen streckt er ferne Vor andern Sternen klar.	Lord Christ, the only Son of God The father in eternity, Sprung from his heart, Exactly as it was written, He is the morning star, His radiance extends to far places Brighter than all other stars.

Elisabeth Cruciger, 1524

According to recent research, Bach during his Leipzig period, and possibly as late as 1740, authored a cycle of eight chorale fughettas (BWV 696–9 and 701–4) for the seasons of Advent, Christmas, and New Year. In a chorale fughetta normally the first chorale phrase is set as a short fugue, for the hands alone, but in these eight works, henceforth cited as the 'Leipzig fughettas', additional phrases of the hymn are sometimes incorporated as well, leading to some of the composer's most imaginative and sophisticated keyboard music altogether.

A case in point—and a work whose buoyancy belies its complexity—is this three-voice arrangement of Elisabeth Cruciger's Advent hymn. Bach treats his fugue subject, derived from the first phrase of the chorale, ordinarily enough for the first three statements, but already in bar 3 the free countersubject enters prematurely; in bars 8–10 the second phrase of the hymn tune is implied in the top voice. The two phrases are then stated simultaneously, cadencing together on the downbeat of bar 13, and then, in the top voice and embedded within a final flurry of semiquavers, successively (bars 15–19). During this embellished statement of phrase 1 the bottom voice hints at phrase 2 in diminution (bar 16), and during that of phrase 2 the middle voice presents an unadorned version of phrase 1. An embarrassment of riches in twenty bars of music.

12. Prelude in D major, BWV 936

See note to No. 6.

13. Nun ruhen alle Wälder, BWV 756

Nun ruhen alle Wälder,	All the forests are resting,
Vieh, Menschen, Städt und Felder,	Livestock, people, towns and fields,
Es schläft die ganze Welt;	The whole world is sleeping;
Ihr aber, meine Sinnen,	But for you, my senses,
Auf, auf, ihr sollt beginnen,	It is time to wake up and start work on
Was eurem Schöpfer wohlgefällt.	Whatever pleases your Creator.

Paul Gerhardt, 1648

If genuine, this is a much earlier specimen by Bach of the chorale fughetta. The first phrase of the hymn tune, which derives from Heinrich Isaac's 'Innsbruck, ich muss dich lassen', functions as the subject, whose last statement (bars 12–14) coincides with a shift from three- to four-voice texture. Rounding off this vignette is the final phrase of the chorale, presented in the soprano (bars 16–19).

14. Lob sei dem allmächtigen Gott, BWV 704

Lob sei dem allmächtigen Gott,	Praise to almighty God,
Der unser sich erbarmet hat,	Who took pity on us,
Gesandt sein allerliebsten Sohn,	And sent his beloved son,
Aus ihm geboren im höchsten Thron.	Born of him who is on the highest throne.

Michael Weisse, 1531

Another of the Leipzig fughettas, this relatively straightforward

work also takes as its subject the hymn's opening phrase, which here differs significantly from the Advent plainsong ('Conditor alme siderum') on which it is based. The theme sounds six times, and the final cadence on A represents a modal inflection suggested by the original chant.

15. Nun freut euch, lieben Christen gmein, BWV 755

Nun freut euch, lieben Christen gmein	Dear Christians, let us rejoice together
Und lasst uns fröhlich springen,	And let us leap with joy,
Dass wir getrost und all in Ein	We sing confidently and united
Mit Lust und Liebe singen:	With passion and love:
Was Gott an uns gewendet hat,	About what God has done for us,
Und seine süsse Wundertat	And his sweet miracle
Gar teur hat ers erworben.	That came at such a high price.

Martin Luther, 1523

Also transmitted as 'Es ist gewisslich an der Zeit', this piece loosely conforms to a type of organ chorale associated with Johann Pachelbel in which each phrase of the tune is set as a point of imitation before being stated in augmentation by the soprano voice. Such 'pre-imitation' occurs here only for the first phrase, although the imitative theme itself recurs in bars 11–13 and 54–6; the fourth phrase is foreshadowed in the upper voice of bars 46–7. This less-than-strict methodology has suggested the Gehren organist Johann Michael Bach (father of J. S. Bach's first wife, Maria Barbara) as the composer, but an attribution to the young Johann Sebastian agrees with the surviving manuscripts. The plagal cadence, in conjunction with parallel sixths and the addition of a fourth voice, is utterly conventional.

16. Prelude in C major, BWV 943

Based on a theme similar to that which commences the Canonic Variations on 'Vom Himmel hoch', BWV 769, this imitative fantasy makes a worthy companion to Bach's Three-Part Inventions. As in the composer's mature keyboard fugues, the element of contrapuntal artifice is reserved for the second half, where the theme is simultaneously inverted and stated in stretto (bars 28–9 and 47–50). The harsh ninth chord in the middle of bar 51 may give pause, but any argument against Bach's authorship seems ill-advised.

17. Fughetta in G major, BWV 902

This early, abbreviated version of the Fugue in G major from Book 2 of the *Well-Tempered Clavier* is ostensibly in three independent voices, but the texture often approaches melody with chordal accompaniment—reflecting how fugues were improvised at the time? The combination of constant semiquavers and frequent seventh chords (such as the three stated as a sequence of arpeggios within the subject) bespeaks the influence of Vivaldi's concertos. Before revising the movement for inclusion in the *Well-Tempered Clavier*, Bach appears to have paired it with two different preludes, one (BWV 902a) similar in character and length to the fughetta and another (BWV 902) in full-blown sonata form. Which prelude came first is unclear.

18. Herr Jesu Christ, dich zu uns wend, BWV 726

Herr Jesu Christ, dich zu uns wend,	Lord Jesus Christ, turn to us,
Dein Heilgen Geist du zu uns send!	Send your Holy Spirit to us!
Mit Hilf und Gnad, Herr, uns regier	Rule us, Lord, with love and mercy
Und uns den Weg zur Wahrheit führ.	And lead us on the path to truth.

attrib. Wilhelm von Sachsen-Weimar, 1651

The homophonic texture, boldly chromatic harmonies, and use of rhapsodic figuration between the phrases of the hymn label this piece as one of Bach's 'Arnstadt Congregational Chorales', a handful of works alleged by modern scholars to have thoroughly confused Bach's congregation in Arnstadt when he employed them as hymn accompaniments. Whether or not there is any truth to this notion, the crudeness of some of these harmonies implies that the work could indeed be as early as the composer's Arnstadt period (1703–7). Observe, too, the free voice leading in bars 5–6, where the texture is pared down to three voices and then thickened to six. The chorale itself was sung in various cities on most Sundays as a response to the pastor's pulpit greeting and call to prayer.

19. Allein Gott in der Höh sei Ehr, BWV 677

For verse and translation, see No. 5.

In 1739 Bach published Part 3 of his *Clavierübung*, a collection devoted primarily to almost twenty organ chorales on the German Mass (that is, the Kyrie and Gloria hymns sung at the beginning of the Lutheran service) and the five articles of Luther's Small Catechism. Except for the present chorale, which is the basis for three different arrangements, each hymn is set twice, first with pedal and then without. Designated in the original print as a *fugetta*, this masterful rendition of the Gloria constitutes a compact double fugue whose two subjects are first given their own expositions (bars 1–7 and 7–16, starting with the middle voice) and then combined (bars 17–20); three-voice texture is strictly maintained. The two subjects are based on the first two phrases of the hymn, respectively, and they complement each other with regard to contour (disjunct versus conjunct) and articulation (staccato versus legato).

20. Nun freut euch, lieben Christen gmein, BWV 734

For verse and translation, see No. 15.

Despite the tradition of playing the tenor chorale tune on the pedals, this work is entirely performable hands alone. Indeed, the manuscript prepared by the alleged Bach pupil Johann Christoph

Oley carries the designation *manualiter*, and the piece has been successfully transcribed by such pianists as Ferruccio Busoni. Surrounding the hymn melody is a ritornello in nonstop semiquavers (derived from the first phrase of the chorale) and a walking bass. Never has Luther's joyous Advent message been proclaimed with greater ebullience or ingenuity.

21. Adagio (2nd movement of Concerto in A minor, after Vivaldi), BWV 593

Bach made solo keyboard transcriptions of five of the twelve concertos from Vivaldi's *L'Estro armonico* ('The Harmonic Whim'), Op. 3, published in 1711/12. (He adapted from that set a sixth concerto for four harpsichords and orchestra.) Most of these arrangements appear to date from the latter half of Bach's tenure as court organist in Weimar, where he served from 1708 to 1717 and where he is thought to have written most of his organ music. According to Bach's obituary, the ruler of that court (Duke Wilhelm Ernst) not only appreciated Bach's playing but 'fired him with the desire to try every possible artistry in his treatment of the organ'. The awesome diversity of Bach's Weimar organ works, which encompass everything from flashy concerto transcriptions to sombre chorale settings, bear eloquent witness to this statement.

This hauntingly beautiful Adagio is adapted from a concerto for two violins (Op. 3, No. 8) whose first and third movements Bach arranged for manuals and pedals. Two different manuals are specified, one representing the ripieno, or accompanying orchestra, and another the concertino, or soloists. These transcriptions often contain material of Bach's own conception—thus they represent an exercise in recomposition as well as transcription—but he was content here to make a host of relatively cosmetic changes, such as transposing bars 9–12 down an octave for the sake of a varied restatement of the previous four bars. Likewise, he often chose during the second half of the movement to invert the two solo parts, a technique that in bar 29 avoids a high pitch (d′′′) that was unavailable on the Weimar court organ and that in bars 32–40 creates an alternation between parallel thirds and sixths, as opposed to an uninterrupted succession of the former. Arguably, therefore, Bach improved on his model.

22. Vater unser im Himmelreich, BWV 683

Vater unser im Himmelreich,	Our Father in heaven,
Der du uns alle heissest gleich	You ask all of us to be
Brüder sein und dich rufen an,	Brothers and to call out to you,
Und willst das Beten von uns han:	And you wish to receive prayers from us:
Gib, dass nicht bet allein der Mund,	Grant that we pray not only with our lips,
Hilf, dass es geh von Herzens grund.	But help us to pray from the bottom of our heart.

Martin Luther, 1539

Taken from Part 3 of Bach's *Clavierübung*, this chorale represents Luther's versification of The Lord's Prayer. Bach arranged the hymn here as a melody chorale, with the entire, unadorned chorale tune stated as a continuous melody in the soprano, supported by motivically unified figuration in the lower three voices. The chromatic passing tone on C sharp (see bar 9) also appears in Bach's setting of this hymn in the *Orgelbüchlein*. Whereas that much earlier collection contains over thirty melody chorales, the present work is the only such example in the *Clavierübung*. It may be the last specimen of this relatively simple chorale type that Bach ever wrote.

23. Wer nur den lieben Gott lässt walten, BWV 691

Wer nur den lieben Gott lässt walten	Whoever surrenders control to God alone
Und hoffet auf ihn allezeit,	And places hope in him at all times,
Den wird er wunderbar erhalten	Will be wonderfully sustained by him
In aller Not und Traurigkeit,	Through all need and sadness,
Wer Gott, dem Allerhöchsten, traut,	Whoever trusts in the most high God,
Der hat auf keinen Sand gebaut.	Has not built foundations of sand.

Georg Neumark, 1641

Whether writing for keyboard or voices, Bach was frequently drawn to Georg Neumark's most famous hymn, and three settings are included in the present edition. The first (BWV 691) comes from the *Clavierbüchlein vor Wilhelm Friedemann Bach*, a volume presented by Bach to his son Wilhelm Friedemann on the boy's tenth birthday in 1720. One of the first works entered by Sebastian Bach into this manuscript (Friedemann inscribed many others), its uppermost voice contains virtually all the symbols from the table of ornaments positioned by Sebastian two folios earlier. Sebastian's purpose for selecting such a piece was surely to enhance the youngster's religious education as well as show him how to embellish a cantus firmus. That the work was a family favourite is suggested by its inclusion in the *Clavierbüchlein* presented by Bach in 1725 to his second wife, Anna Magdalena. She was also the copyist in that instance, notating slightly fewer ornaments than her husband had.

In the expanded version of this work catalogued as BWV 691a (No. 24) a lengthy ritornello is added to the mix. To judge from the overtly galant style of this theme, which sounds at the beginning and end as well as between the phrases of the chorale, whoever fashioned this arrangement was born decades after J. S. Bach. Friedemann Bach comes to mind for obvious reasons, but so does his younger brother Carl Philipp Emanuel, who inherited his stepmother's *Clavierbüchlein* after her death in 1760 and saw fit to add the attribution 'von J. S. Bach' to her entry of BWV 691. Furthermore, Emanuel is almost certainly responsible for an adaptation of the *Orgelbüchlein* chorale 'Ich ruf zu dir, Herr Jesu Christ' (BWV Anh. 73) carried out in much the same way.

Bach must have been thinking in terms of dance music when he composed the third setting of 'Wer nur' (BWV 690) printed here (No. 26). In highly unusual fashion, he chose to repeat the Abgesang as well as the Stollen of the chorale, thus creating the same binary form (AABB) associated with baroque dances, and he kept closely to the four-bar phrase structure so typical of those movements—even if he also extended the cadence of each phrase by a bar. Perhaps he set out specifically to simulate the courante, a dance type characterized by triple metre and running figuration (and a moderately fast tempo). The figuration in this case results from virtually constant statements of one of the most common rhythmic motives in baroque keyboard music: three off-the-beat

semiquavers or quavers followed by a fourth note of equal or greater value, and cited by contemporaneous theorists as the *suspirans*, because it begins with a rest or 'suspiration'. The motive appears here in its most common melodic guise: stepwise, scalar motion.

24. Wer nur den lieben Gott lässt walten, BWV 691a

See note to No. 23.

25. Erbarm dich mein, o Herre Gott, BWV 721

Erbarm dich mein, o Herre Gott,	Have pity on me, O Lord God,
Nach deiner grossn Barmherzigkeit,	In your great mercy,
Wasch ab, mach rein mein Missetat,	Wash away and make clean my wrongdoing,
Ich kenn mein Sünd und ist mir leid.	I acknowledge my sin and I am sorry for it.
Allein ich dir gesündigt hab,	I have sinned against you alone,
Das ist wider mich stetiglich;	And this confronts me all the time,
Das Bös vor dir nicht mag bestahn,	Evil cannot exist in your presence,
Du bleibst gerecht, ob du urteilst mich.	You remain just in your judgement of me.

Erhart Hegenwalt, 1524

This work is doubly unique, for it is Bach's only organ arrangement of this hymn and his only organ chorale whose accompaniment consists exclusively of repeated chords. In adopting this texture—and in stating the hymn tune in the highest register—he was very likely influenced by the second movement of a cantata on this same chorale by the Estonian organist Ludwig Busbetzky (d. 1699). Because Busbetzky had trained under Dietrich Buxtehude, it stands to reason that Bach got to know this cantata during his own studies with Buxtehude in the winter of 1705–6. The many seventh and ninth chords in Bach's setting continue to the final cadence, where a leading-tone diminished-seventh chord occurs simultaneously with the tonic pitch. One searches in vain for another organ composer around 1700 who was so fond of this manifestly dissonant combination.

26. Wer nur den lieben Gott lässt walten, BWV 690

See note to No. 23.

27. Christum wir sollen loben schon, BWV 696

Christum wir sollen loben schon,
Der reinen Magd Marien Sohn,
So weit die liebe Sonne leucht
Und an aller Welt Ende reicht.

Martin Luther, 1524

We shall praise Christ,
The son of the pure maiden Mary,
As far as the dear sun shines,
And reaches to the remotest end
    of the world.

Like Nos. 11 and 14 of the present edition, this piece belongs to the collection now known as Bach's Leipzig fughettas. It opens with a four-voice fugal exposition in ascending order, then continues with an episode (bars 11–13) and two more fugal entries at the octave. The cadence on E reflects the Phrygian cadence at the end of the chorale melody.

28. Nun komm, der Heiden Heiland, BWV 699

Nun komm, der Heiden Heiland,
Der Jungfrauen Kind erkannt!
Des sich wundert alle Welt,
Gott solch Geburt ihm bestellt.

Martin Luther, 1524

Come, saviour of the heathens,
Recognized as the virgin's child!
May the whole world marvel,
That God ordained such a birth
    for him.

Another of the Leipzig fughettas, this work begins with a three-voice exposition in descending order, then continues with an episode (bars 7–10), a final entry whose chromatic passing tone on A flat involves a modulation from G minor to C minor (bars 10–12), and a final episode.

29. Vater unser im Himmelreich, BWV 737

This bit of juvenilia begins with imitative statements of the first phrase of the chorale, then evolves into what is basically a four-part harmonization with interludes. Two different three-note figures, either beginning or ending off the beat with a pair of quavers, provide motivic unity. Bach's kinsman and colleague Johann Gottfried Walther equated such rhythms to metrical feet in classical poetry. Thus he considered the pattern of long-short-short to be a dactyl, and that of short-short-long an anapest. For chorale melody and text, see No. 22.

30. Jesus, meine Zuversicht, BWV 728

Jesus, meine Zuversicht
Und mein Heiland, ist im Leben;
Dieses weiss ich, sollt ich nicht
Darum mich zufrieden geben,
Was die lange Todesnacht
Mir auch für Gedanken
    macht.

Luise Henriette von Oranien, 1649

Jesus, who is my assurance
and my saviour, is alive;
I know this to be true, so I shall
take confidence from this,
Whatever thoughts take hold of me
In the long night of death.

Bach penned this miniature, his only keyboard setting of this Easter hymn, into the *Clavierbüchlein* that he gave his spouse Anna Magdalena in 1722. The volume may have been a wedding gift of sorts, since the couple had been married only since December of

1721. As in No. 23, the hymn tune is profusely embellished above two relatively slow accompanimental voices.

31. Gelobet seist du, Jesu Christ, BWV 722

Gelobet seist du, Jesu Christ,
Dass du Mensch geboren bist

Von einer Jungfrau, das ist wahr;
Des freuet sich der Engel Schar.
Kyrieleis!

Martin Luther, 1523

Let us praise you, Jesus Christ,
Because you were born a human
    being
From a virgin, this is true;
Causing the host of angels to rejoice.
Lord have mercy!

Another of the Arnstadt Congregational Chorales (see No. 18), and one of four Christmas hymns in the group, this piece is distinguished mainly by its homophonic texture, wild harmonies, and bravura interludes between the phrases of the chorale. For whatever reasons, though, Bach here dispenses with an interlude between the last two phrases and accompanies the final phrase not with more full-fisted chords but with figuration based on the *suspirans* motive (see No. 26). In contrast to the standard chorale melody, used by Bach on several other occasions (see No. 32), the antepenultimate note of the first phrase is B rather than C.

32. Gelobet seist du, Jesu Christ, BWV 697

This unusually compact setting features twelve statements of the fugue subject—it is absent only in bar 4—that fall into three groups of four statements each: an opening exposition in the tonic and dominant (bars 1–6), a middle exposition beginning in D major and rising by fourths to F major (bars 6–10), and a final exposition in which the subject is varied both melodically and rhythmically (bars 10–14). Comprising the countersubject are two descending scales, which in bar 8 are split between the alto and soprano; in bars 10 and 14 the second scale is inverted. The mixolydian cadence derives from the chant-based chorale melody. For chorale melody and text, see No. 31.

33. Vom Himmel hoch, da komm ich her, BWV 701

Vom Himmel hoch, da komm ich
    her.
Ich bring euch gute neue Mär,
Der guten Mär bring ich so viel,
Davon ich singen und sagen will.

Martin Luther, 1535

I have come down from heaven
    above,
Bringing you good news,
I bring so much good news,
I want to sing and tell of it.

Just like No. 32, this is a Leipzig fughetta based on a Christmas chorale, and in both Bach may have intended to depict the angels at the Nativity through continuous semiquaver scales. Structurally, the present work is even more complex than No. 11, for in the span of twenty-seven bars all four phrases of Luther's hymn are subjected to contrapuntal display. Phrase 1 serves as the main theme, yet it is always accompanied by one of the other three.

This pairing may not be obvious in the opening exposition, but the running semiquavers in bars 1–5 and 8–10 constitute multiple statements in double diminution of phrase 4. As if to clarify his intentions here, Bach also presents phrase 4 in augmentation in the top voice as a kind of interlude between the second and third fugal entries (bars 5–8). Once the exposition ends, phrase 2 makes its initial appearance, first in stretto with itself (bars 10–11) and then simultaneously with phrase 1 (bars 12–15); it is always stated in diminution. Phrase 3, likewise stated in diminution, follows as the countermelody in bars 15–16 and as its own point of imitation in bars 17–19. Bars 20–2 contain a single statement of phrase 1 during which phrases 2 and 3 sound in succession; what is more, phrase 3 is stated in stretto. To conclude, phrase 1 is accompanied only by phrase 3 (bars 24–6). The four chords at the end provide a charming, homophonic contrast.

34. Herzliebster Jesu, was hast du verbrochen, BWV 1093

Herzliebster Jesu, was hast du verbrochen,
Dass man ein solch scharf Urteil hat gesprochen?
Was ist die Schuld? In was für Missetaten
Bist du geraten?

Beloved Jesus, what wrong have you done,
That such a harsh judgement has been passed against you?
What is the guilt? What kind of crimes
Have you committed?

Johann Heermann, 1630

In late 1984 a Harvard professor (Christoph Wolff) announced that he had discovered on the campus of Yale University an anthology of organ chorales compiled by the organist Johann Gottfried Neumeister (1757–1840). Various composers were represented, but by far the most interesting contents of the manuscript were thirty-three completely unknown works by the young J. S. Bach. Printed here is one of the most compelling of the 'Neumeister' chorales. The chorale melody appears in the soprano, supported by motivic figuration in the lower three voices that by the final phrase (bars 32–7) has accelerated to constant semiquavers. Bach's insertion of chromatic passing tones into the hymn tune at bar 33, which no doubt symbolizes the mournful text, allows him—in a remarkable preview of nineteenth-century practice—to write two pairs of chromatic-mediant chords in the order A major, C major, G major, and B flat major. Foreshadowing this passage is the chromatically rising figure in the preceding interlude (bars 29–31).

35. Allegro (1st movement of Concerto in F major, after Vivaldi), BWV 978

In this transcription from Vivaldi's L'Estro armonico (see also No. 21) Bach took as his model a concerto for violin in G major (Op. 3, No. 3). He chose to transpose the work down a step presumably because of the many high Ds in the solo violin part (as was the case with the organ played by Bach in Weimar, most keyboards at the time extended only to high C). He also completely rewrote Vivaldi's continuo line, which consists largely of repeated quavers. For example, the imitative descending scale in the second bar of the ritornello was all Bach's idea (Vivaldi merely wrote crotchets). In the final ritornello statement, starting in bar 60, the scale begins two beats earlier and is followed immediately by a second one stated an octave lower. Such panache brings to mind the very similar elaboration of the ritornello within the first

movement of Bach's so-called Italian Concerto, BWV 971, just as the contrary-motion scales in bars 28–9 recall a passage near the end of that ritornello. Considering also that both works are in F major, these correspondences may be more than coincidental.

36. Fugue in C major, BWV 952

This piece is strikingly similar in its figuration and structure to two other three-voice manualiter fugues in C major by Bach: BWV 870a, which was revised for inclusion in Book 2 of the Well-Tempered Clavier, and BWV 953, which appears to have been composed directly into the Clavierbüchlein vor Wilhelm Friedemann Bach. For unknown reasons the present fugue never became part of a larger collection. Its subject consists exclusively of semiquavers, thus accounting for the perpetual motion in that rhythm throughout. Of particular interest is the statement in bars 11–13, which unexpectedly ends with a Phrygian cadence in D minor. The last episode (bars 31–4) contains the same material as the first (bars 5–8), merely transposed.

Appendix: Johann Georg Schübler, Fugue in G minor ('Lass mich gehn, denn dort kommt meine Mutter her')

Printed here for the first time in a performing edition is an arrangement by one of Bach's pupils of the 'Little' Fugue in G minor for organ, BWV 578. Schübler, who was probably born around 1725 and whose death date is unknown, retained not only the subject of Bach's fugue but its main countersubject as well; however, he wrote his own episodes, including an especially effective one in bars 31–4 based on the head motive of the subject and moving along the circle of fifths. By writing only forty-three bars and by decreasing the texture to two manualiter voices, Schübler also significantly reduced the size of his model. Most intriguingly, Schübler's arrangement is subtitled 'Lass mich gehn, denn dort kommt meine Mutter her', a bit of trochaic hexameter that translates as 'Let me go, because here comes my mother' and that perfectly matches the rhythm of the first phrase of this fugue subject. Does this mean that one of the most beloved melodies ever attributed to Bach is borrowed from a folk song?

Bibliography

Dadelsen, Georg von, ed. Johann Sebastian Bach: Klavierbüchlein für Anna Magdalena Bach 1725. Bärenreiter, 1988.

Dirksen, Pieter. 'Bachs "Acht Choralfughetten": Ein unbeachtetes Leipziger Sammelwerk?' In Bach in Leipzig—Bach und Leipzig, edited by Ulrich Leisinger, pp. 155–82. Georg Olms Verlag, 2002.

Emans, Reinmar. Kritischer Bericht to Neue Bach-Ausgabe, series 4, volume 10 (Orgelchoräle aus unterschiedlicher Überlieferung). Bärenreiter, 2008.

Schulenberg, David. The Keyboard Music of J. S. Bach. Second edition. Routledge, 2006.

Stinson, Russell. J. S. Bach at His Royal Instrument: Essays on His Organ Works. Oxford University Press, 2012.

Stinson, Russell. The Reception of Bach's Organ Works from Mendelssohn to Brahms. Oxford University Press, 2006.

Williams, Peter. The Organ Music of J. S. Bach. Second edition. Cambridge University Press, 2003.